POLY PEARLS

Invaluable Wisdom on Open Relationships, Jealousy, Group Sex & Other Spiritual Pursuits

Kamala Devi
Cartoons by Norman Jung

Published by

ZENDOW PRESS

Polyamory Pearls
Invaluable Wisdom on Open Relationships,
Jealousy, Group Sex & Other Spiritual Pursuits
Vol. 2: Sacred Slut Sutras

ISBN-10: 0-9896485-8-3
ISBN-13: 978-0-9896485-8-5

First edition copyright © 2016 KamalaDevi McClure

All the art in this collection was commissioned by KamalaDevi McClure and is reproduced with full permission from the artists. Copyright for the artwork is retained and shared by KamalaDevi McClure and Norman Jung who can be contacted by email: NormanJung@yahoo.com

Polycule Diagram by Tikva at www.KimChiCuddles.com

Poetry: "Never Satisfied" © 2013 by KamalaDevi McClure was first published on www.KamalaDevi.com

"Sex Geek" is a brand used with permission by Reid Mihalko.
Cuddle Party ® is a registered trademark of Atlas Spooned.

All rights reserved. No part of this publication may be reproduced without prior written permission from the author or artist. This book is available at a special quantity discount for bulk purchases for sales premiums, fundraising, and educational needs. For details, inquire with the publisher. Your ethical economic support of the author's intellectual work is appreciated.

This book is dedicated to:

ROXANNE

My Goddess, my Lover, my Bitch. Because your existence on planet Earth, here, now, over the course of all human history, is a seemingly impossible event in itself, but that my equally improbable life events have positioned me perfectly to meet such a woman – who optimizes the evolution of my soul, is an undeniable miracle!

PRAISE FOR POLYAMORY PEARLS

"Kamala Devi is a shining star among the new generation of polyamory teachers and role models. I highly recommend her courageous and straightforward approach to loving more."
— Deborah Taj Anapol,
Author of *Love without Limits* & *Polyamory in the 21st Century*

Author KamalaDevi is like the magnificent Hope Diamond; a one of a kind, she lives large, dazzles and delights, and has healing properties. A nourishing, delicious book, with plenty of spice.
— Annie Sprinkle, PhD.
Sex Educator and Sexecologist

"Few people have spent as much time thinking about, living, experimenting, learning, and teaching about polyamory as KamalaDevi McClure. And it shows in her writing. Each line in this pithy book shares her deep wisdom born of years on the front lines of her life and love as a radical sex pioneer."
— Michael Ellsberg,
Co-author of *The Last Safe Investment: Spending Now to Increase Your True Wealth Forever*

"A lovely visual and verbal treat to snuggle up with! This unique creation is sometimes funny, sometimes contemplative, sometimes sobering, always leading one into a deeper space of awareness. The perfect bedside book."
— Amara Karuna
Author of *Heartbeat Nurturing Therapy: Healing Our Hearts*

"KamalaDevi punctuates the truth with her refreshingly straightforward, often humorous, and sensually-playful Polyamory Pearls."

— Baba Dez Nichols,
Co-Author of *Sacred Sexual Healing*

"This book infuses its reader with wisdom from the First Lady of Tantra and Polyamory. KamalaDevi has been the guiding light of the alternative communities of the non-monogamous and spiritual tantra for many a decade now. We follow her on Facebook, watch her YouTube, grow in her workshops. You'll love it as we of her community love her."

— Sasha Lessin, PhD
Co-author of *All-Chakra Tantra* and a dozen books with Janet Lessin

"KamalaDevi has done it again! in her own undomesticated deva way. She has brought Art, Wisdom & Eros together, to make another record crop of Love, Beauty, and Higher Consciousness. Some of her pointed one lines pierce the mark, go right to the heart, slaying the illusion of Ego, liberating love."

— Kelly Bryson
Author of *Don't Be Nice, Be Real: Balancing Passion for Self with Compassion for Others*

"Polyamory Pearls are an elixir for the heart, mind, and crotch. The sexual and the divine are married again. KamalaDevi's poetry comes in the best tradition of erotic verse, after Anais Nin, Salman Rushdie, Veronica Franco, Ovid."

— SerenaGaia Anderlini-D'Onofrio
Author of *Ecosexuality, Gaia, Eros*, and many more.

"I celebrate Kamala Devi's courage and applaud her advocacy for the Polyamory movement. We were proud to have her as the keynote speaker for Poly Living Conference in 2013."

~Robyn Trask, Executive Director and Editor of
Loving More Non-Profit http://www.LoveMore.com

TABLE OF CARTOONS

Introduction viii

Amory 1

Activism 9

Boundaries & Agreements 19

Communication 29

Community 37

Compersion 45

Free Love 53

Geekery 63

Group Sex 73

Humor 81

Jealousy 93

New Relationship Energy 103

Open Marriage 113

Parenting 123

Pleasure 133

... & CONTENTS!

Polyamory 141

Poly Problems 149

Processing 157

Promiscuity 167

Queerness 175

Reality TV 183

Relationship Transitions 195

Self-Love 209

Spirituality 219

Vulnerability 227

Epilogue 235

Never Satisfied 236

The Superpod 239

About the Author & Artist 247

Acknowledgments 251

INTRODUCTION

Polyamory is but one of my identities – I was tantric, kinky and bi-sexual, way before I had my first threesome. At heart, I am an activist, not promoting any one sexual identity as much as advocating for the liberation of love.

Ironically, I never set out to become the "Queen of Polyamory"; but since the position was open (and non-competitive) I was honored to take the post and serve. I'm humbled by my family's willingness to share their private lives on the first non-monogamous reality TV, Showtime's *Polyamory: Married & Dating*. I'm most proud of how this radical rendezvous with Hollywood made "polyamory" a household term, almost overnight. Huge kudos to the creator, producer and director, Natalia Garcia.

I still get hundreds of inquiries from people wanting more. More details. More love. More naked pictures. More of anything I'm willing to share. So even though I'm stretched between motherhood, my career, and a dozen lovers, I made a practice of posting at least one sentence about the deep matters of my heart, per day, on Facebook. Those little lines added up to several volumes called the Sacred Slut Series.

This book is a collection of multidimensional seeds of truth from my unique poly perspective, which will continue to shift beyond its print date. I do not claim to speak for the entire emerging subculture of non-monogamous lovers. In fact, my style of relating is an extreme deviation from the norm. For over a decade, I have maintained an intimate circle of lovers who all know and love each other.

Polyamory is obviously not the only path. My husband is a swinger. I have a girlfriend that calls herself fluid. And a whole host of post-conventional lovers who prefer not to use labels. Our unique sex-positive community happens to mix spirituality, kink, gender bending, tantra and other queer geekery. My polyamorous peers have criticized my portrayal of polyamory in the media as being overly sex-focused.

The camera has also brought into frame important social questions about diversity and inclusion. As a cisgender, able-bodied, middle class, 40-year-old, Latina woman of Jewish descent, I have particular biases and privileges that are valuable to disclaim. By expressing my deepest personal experiences I hope to touch something universal. I apologize to any readers who do not recognize themselves in this book and may feel marginalized by my choice of words or our art. My collaborating cartoonist is an 80-something, heterosexual Japanese man who is presumably monogamous, and was challenged by my off-color sense of humor. I'm going for political satire not political correctness.

Maintaining a sense of humor about our alternative lifestyle is a prerequisite for all my lovers. I had a blast brainstorming these raw, edgy and sometimes even offensive cartoons. I gave up many hours of sexy time with both Roxanne and Michael to get their help coming up with the original concepts. As a subculture, I believe we poly folk must be able to laugh at our sometimes silly selves.

I hope to transmit the nostalgic thrill I felt thumbing through my parents' hidden *Playboy* collection, pouring over pictures while wishing I understood the captions, before stuffing them back between their well-used mattresses. Finding an old-school illustrator was my biggest challenge. I lost three commission contracts based on value differences because of my lifestyle. At long last, I am delighted to have found Norman Jung, with his retro single-panel gag-style cartoon. He brought experience and equanimity to the job, which was necessary since this is my first stab at creating cartoons. It's not possible to enjoy reading them as much as I delighted in creating them, but I dare you to try.

Ultimately, the purpose of this book is to give people permission to express their love beyond all cultural limitations and to have fun doing it!

Wake up and dream,

KamalaDevi

Love is transmitted in both particles and waves.

• • • ● • • •

In your presence, I open to love, physical or otherwise.

• • • ● • • •

Love is like liquid. There is an infinite wellspring flowing from within. In order to take form, it needs a container. That is what relationships do: they hold the love. Monogamy is the standard issue container whereas non-monogamy must be custom built.

> Stop teasing me with love to get sex, and I'll stop teasing you with sex, to get love.

In love I trust; everything else is but a passing circumstance.

• • • ● • •

Love goes beyond the ability to accept another as they are, to accepting the way they love.

You have touched my being so thoroughly that I no longer recognize myself as separate from you.

He is such a generous lover, it would be tragically selfish to keep him all to myself.

Whether it's by fate, past life karma, stardust, spaceship, or sheer coincidence — I'm grateful we found each other.

Though I have been touched by many, my heart is like a diamond and can only be cut by another diamond, like yours.

• • ◉ • •

Why, with countless lovers that shower me with adoration, validation, and devotion, do I still swoon when I hear you say three little words?

• • ◉ • •

We all want to be loved, but love is not a state of giving or receiving; love is a state of being.

> I finally met someone who loves me the way God loves — without conditions or demands — but somehow it's easier to forgive God for not calling me more often.

I heart humans.

• • • ● • • •

Relationship satisfaction is directly proportionate to how much we accept people as they are.

Love is both relative and absolute. The small love has fear as its opposite. The big love is relative to nothing. It is the white light that turns into a whole spectrum of experience when passing through the prism of the human heart.

• • ◐ ◑ • •

Needing others does not make us weak; on the contrary, it's what makes our hearts grow stronger.

Hey, who do I have to fuck around here to get some world peace? I mean, sheesh!

• • ◉ • •

I am bound to serve liberation.

• • ◉ • •

I sometimes wish I didn't care so much.

A revolutionary lives on the edge of appropriateness.

Sex is not just another cause; it's the cause of all life.

Being pro-polyamory does not make you anti-monogamy.

> For most people, sexual liberation is going to require a revolution. For others, it only takes a revelation.

A common cause can pull a community together more passionately than race or religion.

• • ● ● • •

What's so damn subversive about loving more than one person without lying or hurting anyone else?

Breakfast of champions: I had two scoops of hate mail with my coffee again this morning.

• • • ● • • •

If monogamy is an essential ingredient for a polite society, polyamory could be a basic building block for free culture.

• • • ● • • •

Maintaining multiple lovers is a pleasure too great to be reserved for just royal families, Mormons and professional golfers.

Conditioned in a culture of violence, I've become so intent on stopping the suffering that I've lost sight of my own peace.

•• •●● ••

My mission is to activate the wisdom inscribed within the body — from a time before our sexual and religious practices were divided and persecuted.

I never set out to make enemies, but the path I travel on is steep and uncharted, so I'm determined not to go out of my way to avoid them either.

• • ● ● ● • •

My prison walls may be constructed by my programmed cognitive misperceptions, but the doorway is clearly made of something beyond mind-stuff.

The trick to being a pioneer is to get far enough ahead that you can see a new path.

If the earth, trees and animals could protest, what would their signs say?

If the class of people who play golf cared as much about the environmental crisis as they did about how many strokes it takes to get their balls into holes, we'd stand a chance at planetary survival.

I stand on the shoulders
of pioneers who've been
denounced, displaced,
divorced, or worse, solely
because of the way
they loved.

BOUNDARIES & AGREEMENTS

One must resist the temptation to make agreements out of passion, but from a clear head and centered heart.

• • • ● • • •

As a policy, "No Drama" is both boring and unrealistic.

• • • ● • • •

Being a courageous "Yes" to life is an experience earned through valuing each "No."

I only add relationships that are enhancing to my previously-existing ones.

• • ● ● • •

When we experience our partners as ourself, win-win solutions are the only option.

• • ● ● • •

Before I take offense at how anybody is treating me, I must remember that it's my responsibility to inform them about how I like to be treated.

You're welcome to change your mind, as long as you communicate when you do.

• • ● • •

There exists a sort of psychic agreement field around the rules of dating. If you are going to break with those unspoken expectations, you'd do well to know what they are and communicate about alternative choices.

I practice transparency to the fullest extent possible, while preserving the privacy of others.

Co-creating with the Universe isn't just about contemplating intentions, but crystallizing and communicating them.

My devotion to our relationship is much bigger than my animal impulses which, in a heated moment, might betray our agreements.

> Note to self: Do not make relationship agreements if the real reason you are doing it is to test if your partner really loves you.

I'm a 'Hell Yes!' or a 'Hell No!' kinda person. 'Hell Maybe' just doesn't have the right ring to it.

My body has an alarm system that goes off when a boundary is broken; it never fails. Sometimes it sounds on boundaries I didn't even know I had.

• • ● • •

Overheard: "She's hot. But she's a hot mess. I wouldn't do relationship with her, but I'd be open to a casual encounter. Even so, I'd have to sit down to discuss it first; but then it wouldn't be so casual, would it?"

I took inventory of my boundaries and realized I've been carrying around outdated defenses from a time when I didn't feel as safe in my body as I do now. Big sigh ... it feels sweet to lighten my load.

• • ◉ • •

Beyond the boxes of friends, dating, primary partners, married ... we are, in essence, lovers. The true poly relationship is not a container, but an organic evolving synergistic co-creation.

Agreeing to something that feels like a restriction will end in resentment; but if you compassionately consider your partner's position, that very compromise can turn into a gift you're honored to give.

COMMUNICATION

Truth is my most
fulfilling lover.

If it's in my heart,
it will be on my lips.

Radical honesty is best
practiced in proportion to
your willingness to hear the
truth.

If you want to really hear someone, listen for love.

• • ◉ • •

Just knowing you up-levels the conversation in my head.

Truth is a target between minimizing and exaggerating.

• • • ● • •

There is skill involved in talking to one lover about others. It sounds something like this: Are you open to hearing about my other relationships right now?

If you can't say anything nice, say something naughty.

• • ○ ● ○ • •

When your intention is to do no harm, and communicating does more harm than good, it's time to cease communication.

By hearing how somebody lost their way, you are helping them find it.

• • ●● • •

There's a fine line between practicing transparency and not having the ability to censor yourself; but real friends don't mind when you cross that line.

It's not that I'm not ready for the truth, I just don't know if I'm up for all the bullshit that has to be cleared before the absolute reality of existence is revealed.

I'm not looking for my soul mate — I've found my soul tribe — and we are always accepting applications.

• • ◦ ● ◦ • •

Community service is graduate personal growth work.

• • ◦ ● ◦ • •

My community fits me as comfortably as a second skin.

My most intimate relationship is with a complex network of individuals.

To love humanity is to want for the whole as much as for each person.

One cannot be a truly great lover without some of it spilling over into the community.

The power of a polyamorous community is only as strong as its communication with the newest members.

• • ◉ • •

One danger of creating a radical sex-positive culture is losing appreciation for the wise simplicity of asexuality.

• • ◉ • •

The collective consciousness of a loving community doesn't just have a mind of its own, but a group heart.

Most free lovers are radical free-thinking contrarians who typically don't align with any massive social movements, which makes it difficult to unify the community.

• • ● • •

There exists a holy circle of blessed beings who are open to experiencing you beyond your projections, and thereby reflecting who you are — beyond your own limiting self-concepts.

> I have created an abundant sex-positive community to compensate for the nagging suspicion that I am alone under my skin.

The quickest way to test and temper a false sense of community is to co-create an orgy, and afterwards show up for whatever came up in the process.

We are each like spiders, sitting in the center of our respective webs, with heartstrings extending out to each person we love. The cords thicken as the relationships deepen. Old cobwebs need to be cleaned up or repaired. Nurturing this web feeds us and sustains the whole ecosystem.

We strive to share
and take pleasure in other
people's pleasure.

• • ◉ • •

If you're jealous and resentful of that which other people have, why would the universe give it to you?

• • ◉ • •

I am no less of a person because I can't satisfy all of your needs; in fact I become more of a person when I accept you getting them met elsewhere.

My self-esteem is not based on being the only source of your affection.

My love for you is so big, it includes all of you, even the needs I can't satisfy.

• • • ● • • •

Don't just share — seek to take pleasure in other people's pleasure.

Feeling that you are being loved warms my heart; I don't personally have to be doing the loving.

I grow bigger in seeing you express yourself in ways that have nothing to do with my small self.

When I deepen my love for anyone, it naturally expands my love for everyone.

May I be blessed with the gift of falling irresistibly in love with whomever my lovers are loving.

• • ◦ ● ◦ • •

When you hurt, I hurt. When you feel pleasure, I revel in it. As such, rubbing up against you causes expansions and contractions; it's rather orgasmic.

• • ◦ ● ◦ • •

Compersion blossoms under specific conditions; it's not like you can find a perfect rosebud and push its petals inside out with your eager little fingers.

My girlfriend almost called out her boyfriend's name today during sex, which turned me on even more!

• • •●• • •

My partner is widely attracted to different kinds of women and when he takes interest in another lover, it calls me to stretch the parameters of my love.

• • •●• • •

My girlfriend looks me in the eyes and tells me I'm the one. I know she is speaking the truth because she said the exact same thing to her boyfriend only moments ago.

I haven't lost a boyfriend, but gained a girlfriend.

• • ◐ • •

The love between us is inherently unique, made even more special by sharing it with others.

• • ◐ • •

Undivided attention on a single lover is a gift indeed! Once mastered, sustaining simultaneous attention on multiple lovers provides deeper degrees of practice in loving as God loves.

FREE LOVE

Free love comes at a cost; can you really afford it?

• • ● • •

Love: One size does not fit all.

• • ● • •

Free love is the spiritual practice of loving the One through the many.

> It's not that I can't decide who to love, but that I don't feel I should have to choose.

By questioning conventions of sex and relationship, we further the conversation of love.

> Need-based relationships are seductive to the ego, but relationships based in choice are satisfying to the soul.

I used to want you all to myself, but since expanding my definition of Self, I want all for you.

My freedom expands beyond my past programming, current circumstances and all the meanings I've made up.

• • ● • •

I didn't give up my security for free love, I just gave up the illusion that my security comes from being the only person who can bring my partner sexual pleasure.

I'm free. He is not my prison keeper. He told me he has no interest in either jailing me or liberating me, for that matter. I didn't even have to sleep with him to get my keys back. (But I did anyway, just for fun.)

• • ◉ • •

Heartache is inevitable when our immense capacity to love is reduced to a single focus on just one other human being.

• • ◉ • •

Know the shape of your heart and see to it that your love life reflects it.

I am a representative of a small but growing percentage of the population who, on the question of love, always answer: D) All of the above.

• • ◉ • •

I may not be able to maintain meaningful relationships with all 7 billion people on this planet, but by loving all my lovers' lovers, I am a bit closer.

• • ◉ • •

Freedom implies choice. So Free love means you choose love. You don't love out of obligation or even your own need.

Walking amongst trees expands the reach of my heart ... and ... I am devoted to gazing into the ocean's depths. Why, if my devotion to the trees does not diminish that of the beach, would my love for someone else lessen my love for you?

• • ◉ • •

Love is not proportionate to how long you have known someone, how old they are, or how many lovers one has. How much we love, however, can be correlated to how open we are to experiencing the absolute in relative form.

> When we realize that love is not something we give or get from others — but the very essence of ourselves — only then do we stop seeking to monopolize, limit or control it in others.

That you belong to the Universe is undeniable; I'm just grateful I get to borrow you from time to time.

The way to a poly person's heart is through their calendar.

You can't simply make love plural without changing the rest of your syntax.

Can't wait until my spell checker stops underlining polyamory.

"Polydar" (Noun). The intuitive gift of observing someone's nonverbal behavior and determining their capacity to conduct honest multiple loving relationships.

• • ◐ ● ◑ • •

Polyamory is an effective strategy for anyone who wants to test their emotional capacity.

• • ◐ ● ◑ • •

Multiple partners equals multiple perspectives, multiple personalities, and multiple orgasms!

Since my connections are not determined by the limitations of monogamy, it's increasingly important to cultivate discernment about who to invest in intimately.

• • ◉ • •

Success in polyamory is heart math; it hinges on one's ability to add and multiply their love, instead of divide and subtract.

• • ◉ • •

Questioning monogamy is like taking the blue pill in the matrix; you will never be the same person again.

> Naturally we will react to someone's actions, but a relationship becomes codependent when we are stuck in a loop of reacting to each other's reactions.

Most stereotypes contain a kernel of truth. Poly folk tend to be word geeks? If you want to test this theory on someone, just ask if "limerence" is in their lexicon.

According to some definitions (and people like my mom), poly doesn't just mean "many" in Greek, but indicates having an abnormal number, too much or an excessive amount.

• • ◉ • •

Good geekery must include some kind of disclaimer about how everyone does poly differently because it can't be overstated that my quirky perspective couldn't possibly speak for all poly individuals and/or families.

"Theogamy" (Noun) – Divine Relating. A Greek word meaning the marriage with or between gods. A union to the divine regardless of whether one is alone, with one partner, or with many. Theogamists may embody various aspects of god/goddess including human, animals and/or celestial beings in their devotional practices.

• • ◦ ● ◦ • •

The more complex a system gets the more order it requires. Multi-partnered relationships are not an exception to this deep natural rule by which the Universe organizes itself.

Polygamy and polyamory are almost opposite. In its extreme, polygamy is a pre-conventional obligation to certain fundamentalist churches. Polyamory, in contrast, is a post-conventional expression of sexual freedom.

• • • ● • • •

Polyamory is like permaculture. Maintaining multiple relationships is like tending to a complex garden of desires which requires intelligent systems to optimize growth through the seasons. If you want to leverage your energy output you must learn about stacking functions.

> I'm in a primary relationship with Clark Kent, and enjoy an occasional hot fling, on the side, with Superman.

"Pod" (Noun). Used to describe a small family or school of social marine animals. Dolphins swim with up to a dozen individuals for mating, protection, and hunting; sometimes temporarily join other pods, forming a Superpod for a frenzy of food and play. (Not to be confused with acronyms: Passed Out Drunk, Print On Demand or Payable On Death.)

GROUP SEX

If God didn't intended for us to have group sex, why would she give us more erogenous zones than one person could possibly pleasure?

No spiritual practice helps me realize that there is only 1 love better than lying in bed between 2 lovers.

I celebrate consensual sex as healthy, natural and fun regardless of whether it's alone or in a group.

Group sex is like good soup. You put everything in the same pot, turn up the heat, but you're careful not to overcook it so the ingredients don't lose their individual flavor.

• • ● ● ● • •

We had a hot MFM threesome while fantasizing about having sex in a monastery and called it the "two monk treatment."

• • ● ● ● • •

Group process, play or even sex is never a sufficient substitute for deep dyadic connection — but it may certainly enhance it!

There are certain taboos which, when broken and witnessed, bring wholeness to the observer. For me, group sex is one such taboo.

• • ◉ • •

Those who are too busy proclaiming that "it's not about sex" often miss out on the profound potential pleasure of simultaneously playing with multiple partners.

• • ◉ • •

It's inevitable, sex pushes buttons. Having group sex with strangers is something like walking into an elevator full of people, pushing all the buttons, then walking out.

When it comes to sexual rituals, if you want to heal your mother/father wound, or touch into the hermaphroditic nature of the soul, making love to both a man and a woman simultaneously is amongst the most powerful acts you can perform.

The key to sleeping three or more to a bed in the summertime is using multiple top sheets. And of course, it helps to thoroughly exhaust everyone first.

Is it still considered group sex if we all agree there's only one of us here?

• • • ● • • •

To make love to me requires that you accept my husband, son, and a whole tribe of lovers that are constantly coming and going. For I am not separate from them. Can you embrace a whole community of touch-hungry tantrikas? How about India, and Mexico? — Can you wrap your legs around all of Mamma Earth?

• • • ● • • •

There is an art to sleeping in the middle and I'm determined to master it.

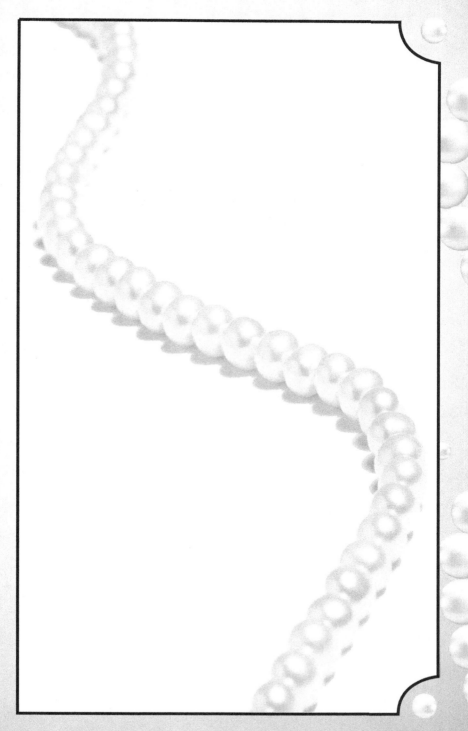

My girlfriend is so poly that when she goes to use her computer at a coffee shop she brings a power strip to share her energy.

• • ◉ • •

Poly folk always kiss and tell.

• • ◉ • •

You can't count poly people in pairs.

Screw the cracker, Poly wants another lover.

Polyamory: More fun than a barrel of bonobos!

Why fish with a pole when you can use a net?

> I'm not polyamorous but all of my lovers are.

Despite the stereotype, not all poly people wear polyester.

• • ◦ ● ◦ • •

Sorry to hear you're monogamous; hope you get better soon.

Why yes, I am flirting with you, and your lovely wife too.

• • ◦ ● ◦ • •

My future self is looking back at me now, shaking her head and smirking.

• • ◦ ● ◦ • •

I'm drying my naked body with un-matching 'his' and 'hers' and 'hers' towels.

I'm so busy with all my poly lovers that I started putting them on my "To Do" list.

• • ◉ • •

I wouldn't be surprised if Earth was not the only planet some of my lovers have lived on.

• • ◉ • •

If there were such a thing as cooties, everyone in my pod would have gotten them from me by now.

My boyfriend told me I had a slutty heart; and you're probably thinking — which boyfriend?

If I were marooned on a desert island — I would never be able to choose between all my lovers!

• • ● ● ● • •

Do bonobos even get jealous? I want to indulge in a degree of freedom and play that rivals theirs.

It's generally not advisable to play leapfrog with a unicorn. However, in the poly community, it might be fun to try it and find out for yourself.

I wish I could walk down the streets proudly holding hands with all my lovers, but the sidewalks simply aren't wide enough.

The only circumstance in which I could justify lying is if the Nazis came to my door and asked me if I were housing polyamorists.

My first experience with bondage was as a kid. After watching Lynda Carter play Wonder Woman, I tied up a neighbor kid and made them tell me the truth.

• • • ● • • •

Ram Dass once said: "If you think you are enlightened, go home for Thanksgiving." I say: "Once you master that, try living in a poly household with four other lovers."

My greatest prejudice against monogamists is how eager they are to pair people off. As if we were socks and God forbid we be left alone in the drawer or all mixed up in a bunch.

· · ● · ·

That awkward moment when you and your lovers step out of the photo booth at the wedding and uncle Rob tells you that the sexy half-naked shots you thought were private will be saved on a hard drive and given to the bride and groom.

Trying to date a monogamous person, for me, is like trying to stuff my three-prong plug into a two-prong outlet — it just ain't gonna fit!

• • • ◗ ● ◖ • •

You can't be poly in a vacuum — well, I guess you could, but that would suck.

JEALOUSY

> To gracefully maintain many loves, the first obstacle to overcome is the notion of a jealous God.

I know I'm not supposed to be possessive — but your ass is mine!

• • ● • •

When people I love are loving each other, why do I feel left out?

I have every reason to brag, but polite society would rather reward me for complaining.

• • ◉ • •

Please don't minimize your experience with anyone else in order to protect me from my discomfort.

• • ◉ • •

If we appreciate humans are more unique than snowflakes, why are we still so envious of each other?

When something is lacking in the relationship or in one's self, jealousy is likely to rush in to fill the lack.

• • • ◉ • • •

Can you engage in pleasure at someone else's expense? And what if that someone insists their pain is growthful?

• • • ◉ • • •

I regularly ingest small but gradually-increasing doses of jealousy in hopes of one day developing an immunity.

> I will not be seduced into the irrational fear that my partner's attraction for other women somehow reflects a lack in my partnership.

The compulsive need to compare comes from deep within the lizard brain, where we still think our survival depends on being the fittest.

• • • ● • •

It takes awhile for the puddles to dry out. Even when I set my mind to stop looping a painful story, the chemistry of jealousy is still in my system.

Polyamory is not the solution to jealousy any more than monogamy is. Sometimes having multiple lovers lessens my insecurity, fear of loss, or feeling left out — but other times it heightens it.

Witnessing someone else's delight as they savor the forbidden fruit is satisfying only when my belly is full. If I am in want, it can be torture.

Watching you with another lover expands me. Now I am big enough to hold two simultaneous but opposite truths: I am elated to see your pleasure, and it hurts like hell.

• • • ● • • •

I feel like I've been in a horrible car crash and survived! Now it's time for me to get back on the road and drive. I'm trembling; be patient with me, I can do it, I just need to take it slow.

The trick to jealousy is rising above the discomfort and recognizing that someone else has what you desire. Instead of condemning them, bless them. Let the Universe know you are big enough to handle getting what you want.

• • ◉ • •

I may sometimes need to be recognized for my uniqueness. It's healthy to celebrate that there is nobody quite like me in the world. But that impulse can suddenly turn sour when it wants to hear that I'm better than somebody else.

Granted, jealousy is complex. The trick is not getting lost in the story. All the specific circumstances can be boiled down to two things: 1) there's something precious you don't want to lose, or 2) your heart is longing for something you don't have ... yet.

• • ●◉● • •

When somebody wants the same thing I want — and is better at attaining it — I can choose to see them as competition, or as my teacher.

NEW RELATIONSHIP ENERGY

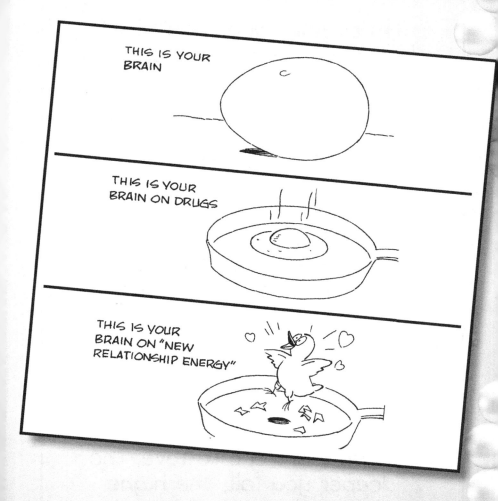

I'm curious what you'll look like when the brain chemistry wears off.

• • ● • •

Together we shapeshift, gender-bend, time travel to become more fully ourselves.

• • ● • •

When leaning into love, the deeper you fall, the higher the stakes.

Falling in love is a dangerous combination of seeing directly into another's soul along with the distorted reflection of unseen aspects of our own self.

I strive to be the version of me that you see.

• • ● ● ● • •

Your touch short circuits all my defenses, but can I really trust you with my tender heart?

There is a place we go, unlike anyplace I've been, a door just showed up and you pulled me in.

Instead of being a contrast to the old, New Relationship Energy enriches the wisdom, depth and passion in all my existing relationships.

There's a thin line between romantic devotion and manic obsession. I don't know which side I'm on.

In my sincere quest to understand the human heart, I stumbled upon you ... and realized ... I know nothing.

• • ◉ • •

I'm glad you don't desire me just for my mind, because I suddenly get stupid when you walk into the room.

• • ◉ • •

I savor the feeling of crushing on you. At times it feels I'm going insane, but sanity never suited me anyway.

What if moths were really angels who burnt off their wings and became human by flying into the flames of love?

• • ● • •

You are like an antipsychotic drug that must be ingested in the appropriate dosage; too much or too little time with you can make me crazy.

• • ● • •

A look from you instantly accelerates my heartbeat; but strangely, a strategically-placed kiss can suspend me to something slower than a stop.

> If it's true that love cannot be created or destroyed, it is just constantly-changing form. Then our current relationship is a new configuration of all the love we've ever felt.

I am possessed with the desire to see with your eyes, touch with your skin, even taste with your tongue. God, it's going to take an exorcism to untangle us.

This love has me inside out, upside down, spiraling like a coin between heads and tails. The deeper I fall, the higher I feel. And everywhere I go, you are there to meet me.

· · • ● • · ·

Can I still call it "New Relationship Energy" when it's with my husband of 15 years?

I feel you penetrating the inside chambers of my heart.

• • • ● • • •

The song on the radio may think it's about love, but if you listen carefully you'll hear: obsession, lack, competition, ownership and entitlement — a poetic cry to fill the hole in the human heart.

I do and I don't.

• • ● • •

We do.

• • ● • •

Traditionally, a marriage license is used like a deed to ownership of another person's genitals.

I am a husband-swapper.

• • ◉ • •

Enjoy extramarital bliss.

• • ◉ • •

My Beloved is the one, but not the only.

When signing our marriage contract, even the minister said, "If your wedding vows involve forsaking all others, I object."

We've shared each other's lovers — that kind of bond runs deeper than buying a blood diamond.

Marriage is a conspicuous and crumbling conspiracy.

The explosion of nuclear households in modern society has caused farther-reaching toxic devastation than some bombs.

• • ◐● • •

My husband loves me through and through. He loves me through sex, through service, through our son, even through sharing me with other lovers.

• • ◐● • •

One of my lovers turns me upside down, another one inside out, several send me spinning, but you are my North Pole who gives order to all my adventure.

Despite the rumors, I am not anti-marriage. I cherish mine so much that I want to incorporate another married couple (and their two dogs) into my nuclear household.

• • ◉ • • •

True love is an act of grace that occurs out of time, giving lovers a taste of the eternal which we pathologically point to with poetry like "until death do us part."

> I'm fascinated by what happens after "Happily ever after," because our marriage is not a fairy tale but a "Choose Your own adventure" story!

Years from now, we will enter into marriage because of our commitment to LOVE. Social pressure, the color of our skin, gender, spirituality or even financial status will be of little concern.

You say I wear my lovers like clothing, and I agree. Each one makes me look and feel differently, and you are like my blue jeans, the ones I wear with everything, the ones I hope I never outgrow because they bring out my best.

• • ◉ • •

Marriage happens in the present tense. It is not something we did, or something that happened to us. If we want to continue to make our lives together, we must perpetually recommit.

An open marriage can be like mountain climbing. You must lean on each other, take turns carrying the baggage, and sometimes double back to rest. High risks yield high rewards. The steeper you climb, the more stunning the view.

• • ● ● • •

Rather than a wife, after all these years of marriage I prefer to think of myself as a perpetual lover.

My father told me his love for me is greater than his prejudice against polyamory.

• • • ● • • •

Poly Parenting is like any other kind of parenting, except you're juggling in a fifteen-ring circus instead of three.

• • • ● • • •

I may know him better, care for him more, and share my whole world with him, but that doesn't make him mine. My son belongs to life itself.

> If most children can adapt to having one parent move out due to divorce, why wouldn't my child acclimate to having more parents move in due to love?

At times, a parent must put their child's needs before their own. Fortunately, a child does not normally need for their parents to have only one love at a time.

> Having offspring is the ultimate reminder that in the heat of the moment, what feels good to the genitals may have irreversible consequences.

Being responsible for the safety of others, most parents strive to operate in the highest good of all, for the longest term, which is a wonderful mindset to cross-apply to our adult relationships in order to minimize drama.

Society is starting to see that the healthiest environments to raise children are ones in which the parents are happy and the children get plenty of adult attention, regardless of who and how they love.

• • ● ● ● • •

Before I got pregnant I imagined that I might become insecure and close the relationship to create a safe little nest for my baby. But as soon as the hormones set in, I wanted to sleep with the entire village that would be helping me raise my child.

They say it's better to have two kids than one. They take care of each other, share, and they don't get spoiled and the love is exponential. Why doesn't this household wisdom apply to lovers as well?

• • ◦ ● ◦ • •

When my producer asked why I want to do a show on polyamory, I told her, because I look forward to the day when my son can point to a show on TV and say, "Look, Mom! That family is poly, like ours."

As important as it is to socialize my son into the world he was born, it seems equally valuable to observe the daily development of this new human animal in order to unlearn my own unhealthy conditioning.

· · · ● · · ·

Society doesn't insist that people only have one kid--claiming that we are only capable of loving one child-- Why does it maintain that we stop at one partner?

Poly Parenting is as much about teaching children honesty, trust and communication, as it is about practicing it with your lovers — regardless of how many you have.

We teach our children to share in the sandbox; shouldn't this still apply in the bedroom when we grow up?

The best teachers of polyamory are parents of multiple children. Watch carefully as they spend special time which each child, motivate everyone's getting along, and are less attached to being the only source of meeting all their child's needs.

PLEASURE

Apologies are not necessary for indulging in consensual ecstasy.

• • ● • •

I am a bliss bunny. Who's with me?

• • ● • •

By nature, pleasure is my first language; everything else is learned.

Damn that dirty little thought that creeps in when we're in the midst of pleasure and says you don't deserve this.

> Being in my body is my favorite place to be, unless there is pain, and then I take pleasure in knowing that I exist beyond this form.

Velvet curtains, stained glass lamps, flavored teas, exotic art ... all in the company of the Beloved.

Hedonism started in the mid-1800s in Greece; hēdon (ḗ) pleasure + -ism. It is the doctrine that pleasure or happiness is the highest good. I say it's time to stage a revival.

You may deem me deviant for openly sharing my heart and body with as many people as I please, but until you can prove there's pleasure in conforming, deviance is working for me.

Escapism does a dangerous impersonation, but I don't let myself be fooled by pleasure's imposters.

• • ◐ • •

It's not that we must learn to enjoy the pleasures of freedom, of sharing, of wanting our lovers to enjoy themselves with others, but unlearn the cultural programming that keeps us from the natural generosity of our spirit.

• • ◐ • •

Pleasure melts the boundary between self and everything else.

At first the impulse is to eat all the fruit within reach. After a few bellyaches, however, the body develops discernment.

> My love life became my wildest dream not as a result of my chasing pleasure, but because I stopped running away from pain.

A woman who has every earthly pleasure imaginable still needs a fantasy to keep her from feeling complete.

Men's nipples may not offer an evolutionary advantage, but in my book, they are evidence that humans are built for pleasure!

• • ◦ ● ◦ • •

Pleasure is a side effect of the soul finding its way into form.

If your idea of romance is adoring someone to the exclusion of all others, I prefer you adore someone else.

• • ◉ • •

There's enough love to go around.

• • ◉ • •

When you are poly, it's less about Valentine's Day — and more about Valentine's Month.

So grateful for my partners' multiple perspectives.

> Polyamory is no better or worse than monogamy, it's just a relationship structure that works better or worse for different people, at different times.

I love my girlfriend! (And my boyfriend loves her too.)

Inherently in loving me you become poly, not because you end up loving all my other lovers, but all my personalities.

• • • ● • • •

Some lovers are so intense, they exclude everything else. I prefer those whose love is so big, they embrace everyone.

• • • ● • • •

It's tragic that people feel they have to sacrifice an existing romantic relationship to explore an erotic attraction for someone new. It's not as sad, however, as the ones who lie, cheat and sneak around.

One of the underappreciated benefits of polyamory is having more people who can bring you soup when you are feeling sick.

• • • ◉ • • •

Some people only have room in their heart for one. Mine is built like a sprawling estate and there's a special suite by the garden, big enough for you and whomever you want to invite. If you don't want it, you'll be missed, but nothing stays vacant for long around here.

> Someone who has cheated in the past is NOT a better candidate for polyamory. However, if they were compulsive about telling the truth, they may have a case.

No, polyamory isn't safe. Life isn't safe. Or fair, or easy, for that matter. But if you want truth, freedom, personal growth — it may be for you. If it's safety you need, don't you dare open your relationship.

Opening to polyamory doesn't suddenly happen when you find yourself attracted to more than one person. It starts with a shift in consciousness. When we realize that withholding our truth dims our light and damages our bonds. It's a whole life philosophy in which love grows when we endorse each other's full erotic expression.

POLY PROBLEMS

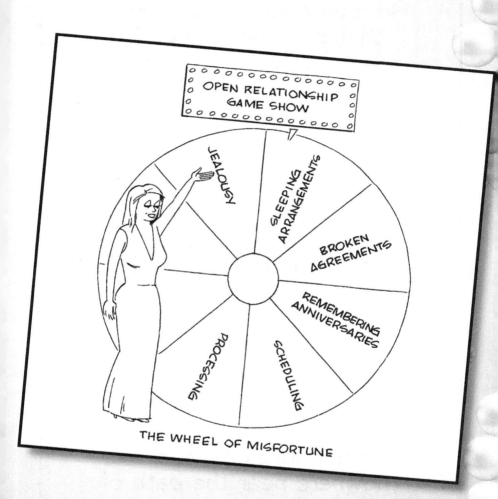

Are you one of those people that preaches about "no drama" while unconsciously indulging in it?

Loving multiple partners is easy. Scheduling is a bitch.

Polyamory has lead me nowhere near the path of least resistance.

Don't lose perspective: Most poly problems are problems of abundance.

• • • ● • • •

Mono/poly is not a board game, but a game of risk.

• • • ● • • •

Easy recipe for chaos: Say yes when you mean no, and no when you mean yes.

After scheduling, the next biggest problem within polyamory is seating arrangements.

• • ● • •

What problems do we have that can't be momentarily melted away by a whole body hug?

• • ● • •

Many polyamorous people lie, cheat and have ugly breakups. It's more a function of their integrity than their relationship choice.

In relationship, we are always in a state of starting, sustaining or separating from another. Sometimes in poly, we find ourselves in several of these stages simultaneously.

Thou shalt not compare, assume, or project thine own judgements.

It's one thing when you're juggling so many balls that you accidentally drop one; it's a whole other story when you're juggling lovers.

• • ● • •

My love, intimacy and sensuality are too immense to be held by any single relationship. Containing my lusty devotion could occupy a small army — and that is on a good day.

The problem with being poly — if there is one — is not between me and my lovers, or me and a mostly-monogamist society, it's not even between me and some jealous god ... it's between me and myself.

• ◦ ● ○ • ◦

If you don't trust that what you bring to relationship is unique and incomparable, then polyamory may not be for you.

Why don't you just ask me about my love life to begin with, because all other conversations we try to start are going to end up there anyway.

• • ● • •

By definition, "process" is always incomplete.

• • ● • •

When in doubt... over-communicate.

How you take feedback is a test of your mastery.

• • • ● • • •

When I have deep and meaningful relationship discussions, they are heart-to-heart-to-heart....

It doesn't matter how we got into this mess, Darling. The real question is: Where do we go from here?

> Hey, here's an an idea: Instead of complaining about how things are not going your way, why not ask for what you want?

There is a bridge that crosses over a lot of egoic bullshit to connect our essential selves; that bridge is called love.

Nearly all the drama in relationship arises from the delusion that we need our lover to say or do something so we can feel that which we already are — love.

• • ● • •

Processing is like sex; it can be passionate, vulnerable, addictive and, depending on your skill, the outcome is either satisfying or frustrating.

As a best practice, don't get off the operating table while surgery is still in progress.

• • ● • •

To dissolve judgment I inquire: What is it about myself, in regards to the person I'm judging, that I am not accepting?

• • ● • •

Perception is altered when filtered through the heart.

> Relationship maintenance is as simple as driving your car into the shop for a regular oil change. If you don't, you're going to break down.

No matter how seductive the drama of life may be, I resolve to raise my vibration to co-create with the writer/director of this grand production.

Stop being a victim of love. It is not something you helplessly fall into. Instead, be an agent of love. Practice it in the most challenging circumstances.

• • ● ◐ • •

Forgive me – when my current communication triggers your past pains and I am confused about the cause. Let me make it up to you by holding you and helping heal those old wounds once and for all.

Saying I'm sorry does not mean that I am responsible for your pain, or that I am wrong. I apologize because I was not able to meet your needs at the time, but now I am willing to listen and understand what those needs are.

• • • ● • • •

When we're able to focus on each other's *god-self*, a lot of the story simply falls away.

PROMISCUITY

A slut doesn't just live outside the box, but enjoys stuffing things into it.

• • ● • •

Through each unique connection with every different lover, I make a wide range of music.

• • ● • •

Sure, some sluts are promiscuous because they're compensating for low self-worth, rebelling against someone else's standards, or just can't say no, but most sluts simply enjoy sex.

Polyamory is not the same as promiscuity. Yes, some people are both, and I celebrate their personal preference, just as I celebrate poly prudes.

> I'm more interested in how a slut wields her ethics than how she looks in lingerie.

Just because I love everyone, doesn't mean I want to fuck them. (But as long as no one gets harmed in the process, I appreciate the freedom to do so if I choose!)

Call me a whore, tramp, nympho or whatever makes you feel more righteous. Such words simply show that when it comes to sex, I have more experience, ease and fun than you do.

Contrary to popular belief, being bisexual, poly, and kinky does not mean I have low standards. In fact it is exponentially harder for me to find someone who will meet my requirements in bed.

Those who are not promiscuous suffer from a greater gap between fantasy and reality than those of us who are.

• • ◉ • •

It's a broken system that says be fruitful but don't be sensual. Unless the mother embraces the whore and the whore the mother, the Earth's offspring will continue to be fractured.

• • ◉ • •

I'm proud of my reputation as a sacred whore whose pimp is the Universe.

Contrary to popular belief, having many sexual partners does not raise the risk of contracting STIs, whereas having unprotected sex with people who don't know or lie about their STI status does.

• • ◦ ● ◦ • •

When an intellectual reads a lot of books, society doesn't say that it cheapens his appreciation of great literature. Why should it be any different for the slut? Indeed each new person we sleep with could enhance our subtle understanding of others, ourselves, and the world we live in.

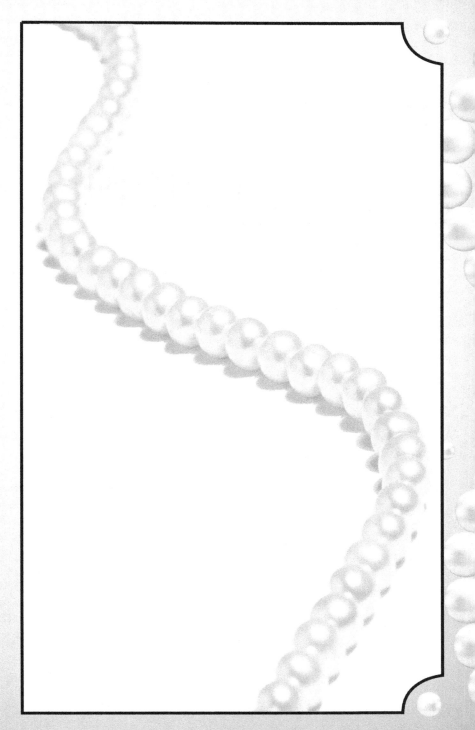

> I admit that same-sex lust suggests a certain narcissism, but not as much as thinking that heterosexuality is the only natural orientation.

I have a thing for men in pearls and women with mustaches.

• • ● ● ● • •

The hole in my heart is shaped like the hole between her legs.

I love men and I love women. If society forces me to make a choice, then I choose love.

• • ◉ • •

As a bisexual woman, the way I see it, if I were monogamous, I'd be missing out on half the fun.

• • ◉ • •

Sappho's words are sweet, but she wouldn't know a damn thing about how to pleasure a modern woman.

Outwardly, I love lingams.
Inwardly, I love yonis.
And sometimes I get so
impassioned I can't keep
them apart.

• • ◦ ● ◦ • •

Power lesbians get more
done because they're not
wasting time with lift-up bras,
skin toners, mascara,
shoe sales....

• • ◦ ● ◦ • •

My boyfriend wants
to write a book called:
Where God's Love Ends.
It's a sarcastic title for
a treatise on anal sex.

We scissor fuck like puzzle pieces that don't actually fit, but leave a hole in the picture so you can remember it's all a fantastic illusion.

> There is an electric polarity between the feminine and the masculine. And lesbian sex is like a double negative that makes everything positive.

Every bisexual woman who marries a man must, at some point, make peace with the fact that he is never going to be a lesbian. I may finally have reached that point.

I threw on a ribbed tank top and asked my girlfriend if she liked how I look in a 'wife beater.'
"That is not politically correct," she protested.
"Sorry; should I have said: 'domestic partner beater?'"

• • • ● • • •

There are rituals to mark the transition from adolescence to adulthood, pregnancy to motherhood, singlehood to married life. But where is the cultural script for celebrating someone's transition into their new Gender Queer identity?

Monogamy and bisexuality are often mutually-exclusive — one usually overpowers the other.

∙ ∘ ◦ ● ◦ ∘ ∙

Being straight and monogamous is not wrong, unless it's by default. Inquire deeper. Join those of us who are not in the norm in defining our own way.

Polyamory is not a spectator sport, unless you have Showtime, Thursday nights at 11pm.

• • ● • ● • ● • •

I'm nothing if not real.

• • ● • ● • ● • •

I'm getting better at pretending to be myself.

Shooting erotica brings new meaning to the word: Action!

The best reality show starts only after you turn off your TV.

The lines between private and public are dissolving around me.

> They can edit the shit out of anything I say, but they can't put words in my mouth.

If Shakespeare were alive today, he might say: "All the world is a reality show."

• • ● ◉ ● • •

Sometimes I wish my life could just go back to normal — as if there was such a thing.

During the span of 2 seasons, the word "polyamory" went from being widely known only at renaissance fairs and sci-fi conferences to being all the buzz at corporate coffee breaks.

• • ◐ ◑ • •

My brother brags about watching my show and doesn't even look away during the sex scenes.

• • ◐ ◑ • •

Did you know there's a little red light on a movie camera that lights up like a clit when it's turned on?

No matter how naked I strip, there still seems to be a veil between you and me. — Maybe it's the television.

• • ● ● ● • •

Can you feel me? Even when framed by Hollywood, and filtered through people's projections, I am still here.

• • ● ● ● • •

You know you're doing provocative work in the world when your fan mail is more disturbing than your hate mail.

I've taken it upon myself to let the community see me fuck up so that they can choose to learn from my mistakes.

When doing an on-camera interview, remember: There's no such thing as a stupid question — only stupid answers.

• • • ● • • •

In not wanting all the adoration to go to my head, I built up my defenses, and now it's hard to take the appreciation to heart.

Want my relationship advice? Next time you get into an argument, set up a camera, press record, then make it public and notice what you learn about yourself. If that doesnt stimulate personal growth, try inviting a camera crew into your bedroom.

• • ○ ● ○ • •

Many poly activists were outraged with Showtime for oversexualizing our lifestyle. But if Jennifer and Tahl were just roommates, they'd be demanding to see more!

One of the side benefits of being in a reality show is that strangers from all over the world feel entitled to write and tell you how you should live your life.

• • ◦ ● ◦ • •

Waking life is so unbelievable, random people even pinch me to see if I'm for real.

• • ◦ ● ◦ • •

My director gave me great spiritual advice: Stop talking about honesty, authenticity, and vulnerability and start showing it.

"We are just like any other family, only we have ten lovers," says my husband to the camera on the first day of filming.

> At times it feels like I am consciously choosing the drama of my life, and other times it feels like the remote control is in someone else's hand; but either way, I am always the observer.

My mother says it's like a soap opera, except she knows the people. ... And then when I call her to talk about my real life she screams: "Don't spoil it for me; I want to watch it on Showtime!"

• • ◦ ● ◦ • •

We have a hard time on date night picking romantic movies to watch because it's rare to find a story that is more interesting than our love life.

RELATIONSHIP TRANSITIONS

I will forever love everyone
I ever loved.

Leave your
relationships better
than you found them.

When your heart feels like
it's ripping into tiny pieces,
look at it this way: you
now have more surface
space to spread around.

If you think resetting a broken bone is a bitch, try a fractured love bond.

• • ◦ ● ◦ • •

Only the fool gives her heart away, then has nothing left with which to love.

• • ◦ ● ◦ • •

My love does not wash away, no matter how many tears I shed; it just glistens when wet.

There exists a sick sort of social stigma on the concept of rebound. The insistence that you have to get over one lover before getting under the next is a symptom of a culture that doesn't understand that the heart is capable of loving more than one.

• • ◉ • •

How about when it's time to detach, we do so gently instead of cutting each other at the root?

• • ◉ • •

Love is like losing your virginity; it only hurts if you don't relax into it, and it can never be undone.

Rebound is the act of rubbing the sensitive new pieces of your heart against someone who cares.

My girlfriend says that if her boyfriend ever broke up with her she would cry between my legs.

Our relationship is deeply personal and widely transpersonal. The trick to breaking up is untangling the personal.

"De-escalating" is not just a euphemism for "breaking up." It connotes shifting over separating. Transitioning can be anything from changing relationship status on FB, taking space, becoming secondaries or even making room for a primary.

> Our love was once otherworldly; now we're worlds apart.

I'm bummed that I cannot love you the way you want, but I refuse to let that close my heart.

• • ● • •

In business, it's common sense to have some kind of an exit strategy when you enter into a partnership. And yet it's considered offensive to even speak of the terms in which you might dissolve a partnership if it doesn't work out romantically.

• • ● • •

You say you still love me, and that's bittersweet because I am still IN love with you.

Unless you consider Rumi's reference to the Beloved, "friends" feels like an agonizing demotion from lovers.

> In truth, the Beloved never left. My body may be somewhere else, most likely with somebody else; but in ultimate reality, parting is not possible.

Being afraid it's going to happen again makes it hard to forgive, but my new prayer is for the wisdom to handle it better should it become a pattern.

Resentment in relationship is like the black stuff on toast. There's a point at which the toast is so burnt, it's not even worth scraping.

• • ◉ ◉ • •

I understand and forgive the defensive impulse to vilify someone you love, when your heart is still attached and the relationship cannot continue.

• • ◉ ◉ • •

Thank you. As a result of the contrast we co-created when we were together, I have expanded myself to the point that I can accept even our separation.

My heart aches so much that I'd rather talk about fashion, weather, sports — anything but love.

• • ◦ ● ◦ • •

If it weren't for my self-righteous judgment and your unworkable personality quirks, we would be spectacular together. Alas, I'll settle for awkward strangers.

• • ◦ ● ◦ • •

One of the rarely-celebrated benefits of being poly is that when you're suffering from a tender heartbreak, one (or more) of your other lovers can hold you, listen, and console you while you mourn.

As much as I romanticize irrationally following the path of the heart, my most devastating mistakes have resulted from allowing my heart and head to travel too far from each other.

Leaving would be easier if there were harsh words, broken boundaries and insufferable dysfunction, but it takes a steeper kind of courage to not settle for comfortable.

When a monogamous couple suffers a breakup, people don't blame monogamy — they give condolences and are sensitive to a mourning period before saying, "There are other fish in the sea." When a poly person breaks up (which rarely happens because they usually just include new lovers and/or transition into best friends), people can't wait to say, "I told you so." and "Isn't it time you got serious and settled down?"

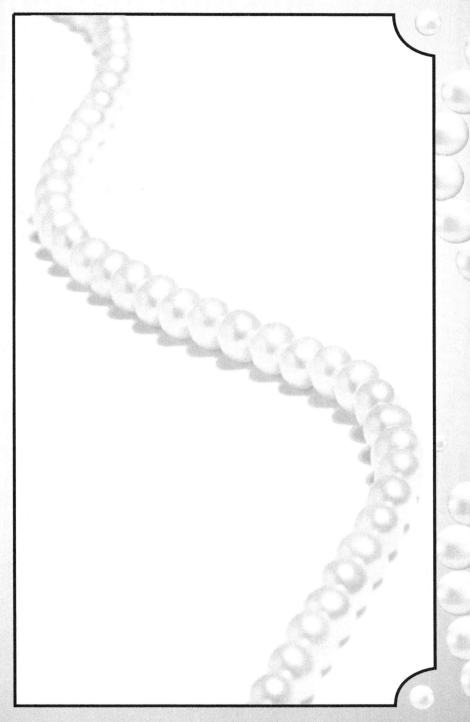

SELF-LOVE

I try not to take myself so personally.

•• •◉• ••

Help! I'm trapped in a house of mirrors.

•• •◉• ••

I am indulging in self, and I feel naughty.

It's not that I'm narcissistic,
I'm just awesome.

• • • ● • • •

You are most lovable when
you are loving yourself.

This is my daily
workout: I rush up to
the edge of what
I know about
myself and push.

Only I can choose whether to act from ego, instinct, conditioning, or love.

• • ● • •

... then life became like a lucid dream, wherein everyone I met was a reflection of me.

• • ● • •

There is no excuse for betraying yourself, not even if you lose acceptance from those that you love.

Real self-love means sacrificing who we think we are so that our soul can perpetually flower through us.

• • ◦ ● ◦ • •

There is something I want you to know about me. As soon as I discover it, you'll be the second to find out.

• • ◦ ● ◦ • •

When I inquire, "Who am I?" I'm not looking as much as gathering inspiration to play the role of whomever I want to be.

Falling in love with the personality may feel wonderful for a while, but it's a trap that does not deliver us to our true spiritual identity.

• • ◉ • •

What good is the impulse to know myself, when I am not who I was yesterday, and who I will be tomorrow is ... unknowable?

• • ◉ • •

Every relationship is a mirror. I surround myself with deep intimate reflections, in hopes that my once-glaring blind spots will melt away.

When asked why
it is so easy for
me to be intimate with
strangers, I answer: To the
degree that I know myself,
there are no strangers.

> When I truly embrace
> my aloneness,
> the Universe hugs back.

You've probably heard that
we can only love others to
the degree we love ourselves.
Now imagine the exponential
necessity of self-love when
loving multiple partners.

To those who want to minimize others so your light appears brighter: Good Luck. Real radiance starts when you stop managing others, and just be you.

• • • ● • • •

I am healthy, abundant, on purpose, surrounded by a like-minded community and devoted family; and still I sometimes feel insecure, broken, lonely, and question my worth.

My purpose is to be me. As simple as it sounds, it involves realizing my essential nature in relationship to interconnected systems such as family, lovers, culture, society, and all of existence.

SPIRITUALITY

Most of my lovers are atheist — some because of a devotion to science, others because of a rejection of religion; but that doesn't stop me from seeing their divinity.

> Relationship is my religion. ... and I'm polytheistic.

I seek to love as God loves — as if there were any other way.

The yoga of love stretches my heart. Your gentle adjustments enhance my asana.

• • ◉ • •

The closer I get to God, the more I want to share myself with others.

• • ◉ • •

Seeking, like trying, is a practice, not to be confused with the way.

I'm on my knees, searching my soul, praying for guidance; and in her infinite wisdom, the Goddess simply says: "Smile more."

• • ◉ • •

Bound to the Beloved, my love is emancipated.

• • ◉ • •

I have 3 primary spiritual practices: breathing, loving and writing. My definition of "primary" is that I'm never not doing them.

> Don't cast stones at me for being polyamorous. Consider how many nuns around the world marry Jesus every day. I haven't a fraction of as many lovers as he has wives.

Forgiveness is the holy practice of accepting suffering as a part of life, without perpetuating it by closing our hearts.

By maintaining multiple deep evolving relationships, I am getting to know God.

• • ◉ ● • •

The human soul is a mystery. It exists beyond the body, it can sometimes be seen through the eyes, it seems to travel in groups, but can get lost then found again in a mate, or a kiss or a stark-naked confession.

Intimacy is scary. It's like letting people read my journals or listen to me singing in the shower. Can they appreciate me as a work in progress or do they just want the polished version?

• • ● • • •

The ego doesn't mind being real, as long as it looks good.

• • ● • • •

Some maps are seductively more attractive than the territory.

If you weren't concerned with making me love you, who would you be?

• • • ● • •

If I could show you that this love cannot be lost ... would you let me in?

The world can only deem us acceptable to the degree that we accept ourselves.

> When I open my heart to loving more people, I also open myself to feeling their sorrow, their insecurities, their longing, their humanity.

I may be strong on the outside, but don't let that fool you. Inside I've got a soft, gooey center.

I am not striving to let go of fear as much as I am working on accepting it.

• • ● • •

Let's strip off every last layer of projection, expectation and attachment. I've suffered so many falls from said pedestal that I've become afraid of heights. I now prefer to be taken, naked, on the floor.

As an infinite being expressing myself in finite form, I get frustrated. There's not enough time. There's not enough space. Somehow my ego then distorted this into the fraudulent belief that I'm not enough.

• • ◉ • •

I used to withhold my sexuality, for fear that people would fall in love with me. But if my full erotic expression inspires love, I no longer take it personally.

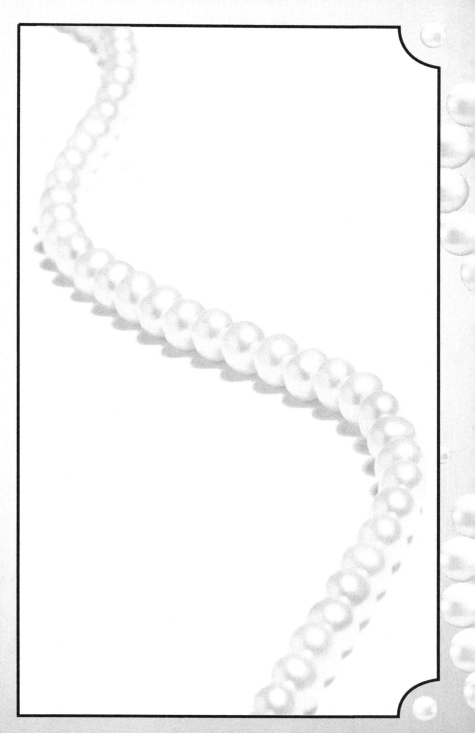

NEVER SATISFIED

Your hand sweeps my forehead
half showing your affection,
half testing for fever.

I may not be measurably sick,
but it's no secret
that I am burning inside.

My heart is always stretching,
my hands are always grasping,
and my head is always, always, always
making meaning where there is none.

No, it's no secret
that I'm not satisfied.
No matter how delicious,
this meal is not my last.

This moment is not the only.
And I know, without apology,
this love is not enough.
Indeed, enough is not enough.

You gaze into my eyes
with a question on your lips
which no amount of kissing
could ever satiate.

This mystery wakes me up
and tucks me in at night,
where the riddles of my dreams
make me wonder even more.

Tell me how our bodies
manage to ever separate,
when merging into one
seems our natural state.

Tell me how come love,
both given and received,
disappears like music
that is never seen.

And if the energy
between us
can't decide
between waves
or particles,
why should I
ever settle
for anything?

No, it's no secret
that I'm not satisfied.

No matter how delicious,
this meal is not my last,
this moment is not the only.

And I know, without apology,
Love is never satisfied.

THE SUPERPOD

JUICY DETAILS

Whenever I travel around the world, people always ask me about my lovers, and how it all works. I often say we are a dynamic constellation of about a dozen heavenly bodies in constant motion. Some lovers are consistently close in orbit, like the moon, while others are farther away, but visit frequently, like recurring comets. This cosmic metaphor paints a vague picture but avoids the vulnerable details.

I've decided to take an artistic risk in this book and actually paint a picture of my constellation. So I commissioned a popular poly cartoonist to draw what she calls a "polycule" or a diagram of my most intimate network. At first it seemed like a simple project, but since many of my lovers are adamantly against labels, it turned into quite the controversy. Since we all share a deep value for organic evolution, they started questioning my motives. Why do I feel compelled to dissect a living organism and reduce our multidimensional dynamics into a few simple lines?

Beyond my own egoic desire to locate myself within this intricate web, I came up with two more reasons. First, it's a sort of love declaration. In a world that doesn't legitimize non-primary lovers, I want to make it known how proud I am to be making my life with the individuals in this poly family. Further, because we are role models and I feel a spiritual obligation to share what we've built for the benefit of the larger community, I intend for this illustration to be used as a diving board for a deeper conversation.

As such, dear reader, please don't skip the disclaimer and the full description of how this complex system evolved. I wouldn't want you jumping to conclusions based on just a cute cartoon.

DISCLAIMER:

This diagram was drawn at a particular point in time. When you read this, the relationships within the Superpod will already have shifted. It's not that we are a particularly unstable group, but we strive to seek right relation which, to borrow a Native American term, means: "We know we are always connected, but it's up to each of us to show up in our higher self and frame each relationship in a way that brings out the best in everyone."

The "polycule" would look totally different if drawn from anyone else's perspective, as every person has their own constellation. I put myself in the center and don't claim to speak for everyone. This picture is incomplete, as it only shows about half of the San Diego Superpod and that is still only about half my lovers. My personal definition of "lover" is not limited to sexual contact, but includes anyone who has a special place in my heart.

These individuals were selected because they are a tightly connected group who were willing to have their name and likeness used. I am so grateful to be among such a transparent group of activists, artists, teachers, and healers who understand that our personal work can raise consciousness for the collective.

At some point, most everyone within this group has had varying degrees of sensual connection with everyone else, unless blood-related or underage. We also have many deep platonic relationships such as siblings, business partners, roommates and co-parents. I chose to limit the relationship labels on this diagram because I did not want to overwhelm the reader or clutter the art. In a future project, perhaps it will be fun to list some other titles that we actually use to describe our relationships, such as:

- Soul Mates
- Erotic Friends
- Saphosexuals
- Non-Primary

- Harem Sisters
- Energetic Lovers
- Sometimes Lovers
- Has Sex at Play Parties
- Dominant and Submissive
- Enjoy Occasional Threesomes Together
- Meet Up for Weekly Sensual Massages

With all the above possibilities, you might imagine how challenging it was for our group to squish our full range of feelings into four simple categories. After many growthful conversations we came up with the following guidelines, and each person selected which relationship best described their connection to the others.

1. **Married**: You've made a public declaration of your life partnership in some form of sacred ceremony.
2. **Current Lovers**: You are frequently in romantic and sexual connection with each other.
3. **Former Lovers**: Your relationship has undergone some kind of a mutually agreed upon transition or separation. (In many cases, former lovers may still connect romantically or even sexually but they have matured into a deeper, more stable bond where friendship is at the basis of the connection.)
4. **Long Distance Lovers**: You maintain some degree of sexual intimacy despite not living in the same city.

Where there are no lines between people, it's because they couldn't squish their love into one of these general definitions.

The ultimate key to this map is simple:

> *Beyond the boxes of friends, dating, primary partners, married ... we are, in essence, lovers. The true poly relationship is not a container, but an organic evolving synergistic co-creation.*

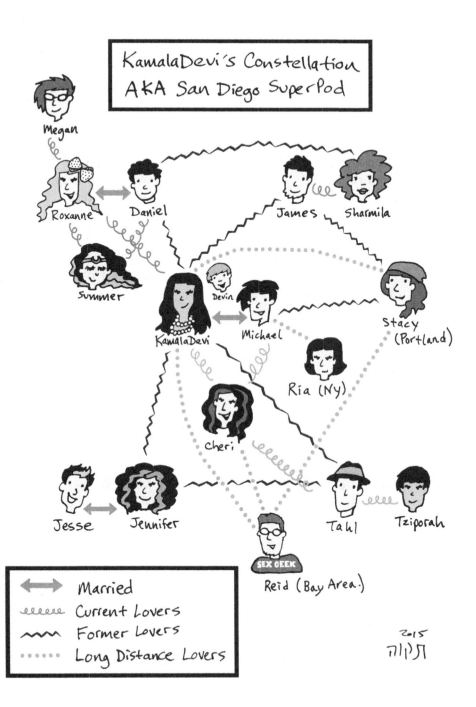

THE JUICY DETAILS:

I've been in an open marriage with my beloved Michael for almost 15 years and we are constantly rediscovering each other. There is tremendous stability in owning a home and co-parenting, among the perpetual changes within our constellation. We both prioritize quality time with our son Devin (now age 9). He has a strong bond with many of our lovers, his grandparents, and his best friend's family who, though monogamous, are supportive of our lifestyle.

Of course, we still face our own challenges such as jealousy, stress and social stigma. Currently, we are still recovering from our painful breakup with Rachel, who lived with us for over a year after the TV show finished filming. Rachel has since been traveling the world and is now living in Sweden, with her Beloved.

At the time *Polyamory: Married & Dating* was being filmed, Michael and I were in a romantic partnership with another married couple, Jennifer and Tahl. Although we all lived together for about three years, so much has shifted since the show wrapped. We have all deepened in friendship, but Jennifer and Tahl have since moved out and got a divorce.

We all recently supported and celebrated Jennifer and Jesse's wedding which was followed by a steam punk themed play party. They bought a house together and we continue to meet up more than twice a week for Pilates, lunch, and other fun outings like comedy clubs.

Tahl and our dear friend Tziporah have been living together in a primary relationship, and we meet up for meditations or to trade healing sessions. The entire family stays connected over frequent vegetarian potlucks, dinner parties and Superpod meetings.

One of our longest-standing relationships has been with Cheri. She maintains that she loves me and Michael, equally. She is a free spirit who doesn't use labels. We've experimented with every kind of relationship style, shared many lovers, and even lived together for a brief time. She recently bought a house up the street and we enjoy weekly writing dates.

For almost five years, my most consistent love affair has been with Roxanne. She is a yogini and pole dance instructor, and we enjoy wild fantasy play, BDSM, as well as meditation. Together we are channeling a book called *52 Fridays with My Bitch*.

Roxanne's husband is Daniel. He is a brilliant evolutionary visionary that used to be my tantric lover before he met Roxanne, but we've since moved into more of an intellectual affair and remain deeply linked at the level of the soul.

For the past several years, Roxanne and Daniel have been in a deep triad with a magical artist named Summer. Summer lives with Daniel's brother James, who was also my boyfriend until about a year ago when he fell in love with one of Roxanne's best friends, Sharmila. Since the open-minded Sharmila is relatively new to poly, James and I decided it best to separate while they build security in their now primary relationship.

Roxanne has also been dating a queer massage therapist named Megan for the last year. This was her first poly experience, so she gets frequent support from the whole family, and has proven to be a quick learner.

This complex system would not be sustainable without a safe place to process our feelings. The Superpod gathers regularly to discuss and clear the emotional issues that arise from sharing lovers. We also travel to study tribal technologies at free-love communities such as ZEGG in Germany and Tamera in Portugal, La'akea in Hawai'i, and Network for New Culture summer camps around the country, so we can continue to learn from past pioneers and further evolve new ways of relating for the future.

With the support of our friend and lover, Reid Mihalko (the original Sex Geek), we've been experimenting with a Free love festival called PolyPalooza over the last decade. It is here that Michael and I fell in love with Ria from New York and Stacey from Portland. And we have maintained long-distance love affairs.

Of course, I also enjoy traveling to teach in cities where we have pre-established relationships with other lovers, some of whom have been with our family for many years. Even though they are not listed on this love map I must mention a few who've deeply penetrated my heart such as Baba Dez, Charles and Christy Muir, and Bruce and Shakara Lyon. Perhaps their stories will be included in my next book.

ABOUT THE AUTHOR

Kamala Devi is a bisexual Latin woman of Jewish descent who was raised between conservative Orange County and a ranch in Mexico. Throughout college, she produced a handful of feminist-themed plays. She founded the first bisexual and lesbian women's discussion group at her university.

Before she even heard the word polyamory, her college girlfriend pointed out that she was in love with a male yoga teacher and she began dating them both... After graduation, she moved to a drumming commune in Hawaii where she was initiated into tantra. In '97 she directed the lesbian, gay, transgender and bisexual Pride festival of Honolulu in 1997. Where she met a professional dominatrix who introduced her to the world of kink.

After a spontaneous sexual awakening on the islands, she began backpacking and studying yoga throughout Europe, Southeast Asia, and China. When she returned to California, she met her life partner, Michael, at a Tantric puja in San Diego.

Together they took a pilgrimage to South India to study Goddess worship from a guru who channels Kali. The 2004 Sumatran Tsunami struck the very beaches where they were at the exact moment their airplane lifted off. This event inspired Kamala Devi's first novel, *Don't Drink the Punch: An Adventure in Tantra.*

When pregnant, they bought a beach house that Michael converted into an eco-friendly temple where they home-birthed their son Devin Echo McClure. He is now an 9 year old bilingual scientist who loves to sail and surf. Devin is proud to be raised in a polyamorous family with a variety of live-in lovers who were featured on Showtime's docu-series, *Polyamory: Married & Dating* which ran for 2 seasons.

Kamala Devi's girlfriend Roxanne is co-author of the erotic novel, *52 Fridays with My Bitch*. Together, they are part of a circle of about a dozen lovers who are transparent about everything. This group is affectionately called the "Superpod."

Kamala Devi is the founder of both TantraPalooza and PolyPalooza, which are annual festivals for free lovers. She also created and directs Tantra Theater, a collective of artists, teachers and healers who offer live performance art to heal sexual guilt and shame. www.TantraTheater.TV

She is co-author of *Sacred Sexual Healing* with Baba Dez and is featured in his award-winning documentary, *Sex Magic*. She is on faculty with International School of Temple Arts. She has made several instructional DVDs including *Earning your BLACKBELT in Relationship* with Reid Mihalko.

Today, Kamala Devi is a highly-visible spokesperson and has facilitated over a thousand sex-positive events in the last 20 years. Kamala Devi has also appeared on the *Tyra Banks Show*, *Discovery Channel*, *Morning Show Live*, *Inside Edition*, and MTV's *True Life*, to name a few. Her future vision is to create a retreat center so people from all over the world can liberate their love lives. Kamala Devi is devoted to helping people liberate love and ethically awaken their sexuality, because she feels it is necessary for the evolution of the planet. She is especially interested in training healers, teachers and visionaries so they can become Love Leaders around the world.

Kamala Devi takes pleasure in nature, massage, vegan foods, snuggling, dance, theater and performance art. Her ultimate turn-on is penetrating conversation. Kamala Devi is a natural muse and uses her body as a doorway to enlightenment. She knows how to use her mouth and words to stimulate and heal people. She is also a deep listener, and loves silence, touch and laughter. For free resources on how to become a better lover go to: KamalaDevi.com

ABOUT THE ARTIST

Norman Jung has been doing freelance art for over 2 decades, from pencil drawings in elementary school to cartoons in his high school newspaper. He sold his first cartoon while serving in the Air Force. Upon discharge, he earned a Bachelor's Degree in Commercial and Advertising Art at San Jose State University. He considers himself fortunate to earn money while doing what he loves! He can be commissioned for humorous illustrations for books, magazines, greeting cards, newsletters, websites, etc. NormanJung@yahoo.com.

ACKNOWLEDGMENTS

Michael, thank you for being rock solid in your support, giving me permission to fly to new heights and dive to new depths.

I'm also grateful to Devin Echo McClure for constant humor and inspiration.

When he was seven years old, I asked him how he would like to live in a hotel with all our lovers.
Devin: "It sounds hot."
Me: "What do you mean?"
Devin: "Polyamorous people talk a lot, and since talking generates heat, it would get too hot to all live in one house together."
And so instead of building a poly hotel, I put my energy into writing this book.

CARTOONS:
I'm grateful to Roxanne and Michael for spit-firing ideas and helping me come up with the concepts. Huge gratitude to Norman Jung for his flexibility, efficiency, and word economy which increased the impact of this work.

POLYCULE ART:
The talented author of KimchiCuddles: Tikva Wolf.
www.Kimchicuddles.com

COVER ART:
After many bizaar cartoon drafts, the cover ultimately morphed into a concept created by Miguel Kagan with a central image visioned by Kimberly Mattegit. Thanks for putting pearls on my heart.

INTERIOR DESIGN:
Huge gratitude to DJ Rogers from JustWrite Design Services for her enthusiastic creative input and keeping a positive attitude despite many late nights of working on nuanced revisions.

GRAPHIC ART ASSISTANCE:
Carol Torrance, & Fiverr/Dorobi and a free hand line drawings by Elsie Lavender, MorlockDesigns@gmail.com and Poly Goddess and Cartoonist Ria Onomatopoeia.

PHOTOGRAPHY:
Back Cover Photo by Julie Kondor. Interior shot of the author by Tantric Rabbi Ohad Ezrahi. Sexy models were pulled from ISTA Level 2 in Jerusalem. Thank you: Bruce Lyon, Dawn Cheri, Xavier Bouquillard, Irena Fridrichová.

GRAPHIC ART ASSISTANCE:
Miguel Kagan for overseeing the creative concepts.

EDITING:
Mary VanMeer, the virtual book goddess who is not only my second set of eyes but arms because she manages my CreateSpace and Amazon accounts.

MY MUSES:
Additional inspiration for various sutras came from San Diego Tantra Theater Players, specifically: Nate Darling, Colibri, & Katie Anne Holton.

And an extra special thanks to Beloved Bruce and Shakara Lyon for transmitting an embodied experience of Theogamy.

MY READERS:
I have no way of knowing who will be magnetized to this body of work, or how it will change our lives, but in the ground of my being, I trust that an evolutionary transformation will come from our co-creation.

WANT MORE?

More by KamalaDevi:

To stay in touch, please sign up for a FREE newsletter with monthly wit and wisdom from Kamala Devi's soul. Simply go to: www.KamalaDevi.com

Sacred Slut Sutras, Vol. 1
Don't Drink the Punch: An Adventure in Tantra
Sacred Sexual Healing: The SHAMAN Method of Sex Magic, with Baba Dez Nichols
Earning Your BLACKBELT in Relationship (DVD), with Reid Mihalko
The Polyamory Roadmap (eBook), with Baba Dez Nichols
52 Fridays with My Bitch, with Roxanne DePalma
The Pleasure Bible, with Marc Gafni

Public Appearances:

Kamala Devi invites you to dive deep into one of her Poly, Tantra and Shamanic trainings which she facilitates around the globe as faculty of ISTA, the International School of Temple Arts. https://www.schooloftemplearts.org

Also, Kamala Devi is available for speaking engagements and select private healing sessions. To inquire about our availability and services please visit KamalaDevi.com or send an email at: Info@kamaladevi.com

Order Additional Copies:

To order additional copies of *Polyamory Pearls* securely online, please visit www.KamalaDevi.com.

Made in the USA
Las Vegas, NV
13 April 2024

88639472R10148